ARTICLE

NEWSPAPER, MAGAZINE, ONLINE

by Sara Gilbert

Compass Point Books ✦ Minneapolis, Minnesota

Compass Point Books
151 Good Counsel Drive
P.O. Box 669
Mankato, MN 56002-0669

 This book was manufactured with paper containing
at least 10 percent post-consumer waste.

Managing Editor: Catherine Neitge
Designer: ticktock Entertainment Ltd.
Page Production: Bobbie Nuytten
Photo Researcher: Svetlana Zhurkin
Library Consultant: Kathleen Baxter

Art Director: LuAnn Ascheman-Adams
Creative Director: Keith Griffin
Editorial Director: Nick Healy

Compass Point Books would like to acknowledge the contributions of Tish Farrell, who
authored earlier Write Your Own books and whose supporting text is reused in part herein.

Library of Congress Cataloging-in-Publication Data
Gilbert, Sara.
  Write your own article: newspaper, magazine, online / by Sara Gilbert.
    p. cm.—(Write your own)
  Includes bibliographical references and index.
  ISBN 978-0-7565-3855-2 (library binding)
  ISBN 978-0-7565-3945-0 (paperback)
  1. Feature writing—Juvenile literature. 2. Journalism—Authorship—Juvenile literature. I. Title. II. Series.
  PN4784.F37G55 2009
  808'.06607—dc22   2008013342

Visit Compass Point Books on the Internet at *www.compasspointbooks.com*
or e-mail your request to *custserv@compasspointbooks.com*

About the Author
Sara Gilbert studied journalism at the University of
St. Thomas in St. Paul, Minnesota. She has been writing
and editing magazines and newspapers since graduating in
1993. She currently juggles a full-time freelance writing
career with taking care of her three children and a frisky
cocker spaniel named Molly. She lives with her husband
and family in Mankato, Minnesota.

Your writing journey

When is something newsworthy? What makes an event, person, or story worth telling to other people? What details are important enough to share in an article, and how can you find those out? As an article writer, you will discover how to answer these questions and to write about them in a way that will make other people eager to read your story.

News stories start with an idea, but the rest of an article can only be revealed through research. Sometimes your research will involve reading other articles. Sometimes it will involve talking to specific sources about the topic. This book will help you learn how to find ideas and then find supporting evidence to write clearly about those ideas. It contains brainstorming and training activities to sharpen your writing skills. Tips and advice from news writers and examples from their own work will also help you on this adventure of a lifetime.

CONTENTS

WANT TO BE A WRITER?

This book is the perfect place to start. It aims to give you the tools to write your own article. You will learn how to report important news stories and write interesting features with satisfying beginnings, middles, and endings. Examples from magazines and newspapers appear throughout, with tips and techniques from journalists and editors to help you on your way.

Get the writing habit

Do timed and regular practice. Real writers learn to write even when they don't particularly feel like it.

Create an article writing zone.

Keep a journal.

Carry a notebook—record interesting events and note how people behave and speak.

Generate ideas

Look for interesting events, fascinating subjects, or people who are doing unique activities.

Brainstorm to find out what other people would be most interested in knowing about that event, subject, or person.

Research the important details about your chosen topic, including the "five W's": who, what, when, where, and why. And don't forget *how*.

Create a list of the important details that might be included in your article.

| GETTING STARTED | GETTING THE STORY | PEOPLE | VIEWPOINT |

You can follow your progress by using the bar located on the bottom of each page. The orange color tells you how far along the article-writing process you have gotten. As the blocks are filled out, your article will be growing.

Plan

What is your article about?

What are the facts about your article?

Plan beginning, middle, and end.

Write an outline.

Write

Write the first draft, then put it aside for a while.

Check spelling and facts. Is it accurate?

Remove unnecessary words.

Does the article have a good beginning and satisfying ending?

Avoid clichés.

Publish

Write or print the final draft.

Always keep a copy for yourself.

Send your article to your school newspaper or magazine, children's magazines, Internet writing sites, or competitions.

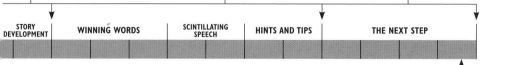

STORY DEVELOPMENT | WINNING WORDS | SCINTILLATING SPEECH | HINTS AND TIPS | THE NEXT STEP

When you get to the end of the bar, your article is ready to go! You are a writer! You now need to decide what to do with your article and what your next project should be. Perhaps it will be another article, or maybe something completely different.

THE "WRITE" LIFESTYLE

Article writers often interview people for their stories. They may do research in the library and on the Internet. They sometimes travel to see places connected to the story they are writing.

Just like all writers, you will need handy tools and a safe, comfortable place to do your work. A computer can make writing quicker, but it is not essential.

What you need

These materials will help you organize your ideas and your findings:

- small notebook that you carry everywhere
- paper for writing activities
- pencils or pens with various colors of ink
- files or folders to keep your fact-finding organized and safe
- dictionary, thesaurus, and encyclopedia
- small, hand-held recorder for taping interviews

Find your writing place

Think about where you as a writer feel most comfortable and creative. Perhaps a spot in your bedroom works best for you. Possibly a corner in the public library is better. If your writing place is outside your home, store your writing materials in a take-along bag or backpack.

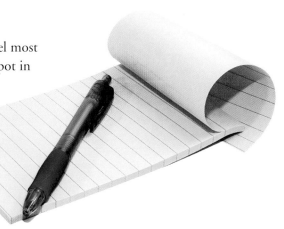

Create an article writing zone

- Play some of your favorite music or music that is relevant to the news story you are writing about.
- Use earplugs if you write best when it is quiet.
- Decorate your space with pictures of your subject or pictures of places or objects important to that subject.
- Place objects that hold good memories from your own life around your space.

Follow the writer's golden rule

Once you have chosen your writing space, go there regularly and often. It is all right to do other kinds of writing there—such as a diary or letters or fiction—as long as you *keep on writing*!

CASE STUDY

California freelance writer Brad Herzog works in a small building next to his home. On the walls, he has framed copies of articles he has written and awards he has won. "A lot of the stuff I have hanging up is there to remind me that I am a pretty good writer," he explains. "That helps give me confidence when I'm writing. The most important thing a writer can have is confidence."

STORY DEVELOPMENT	WINNING WORDS	SCINTILLATING SPEECH	HINTS AND TIPS	THE NEXT STEP

GET THE WRITING HABIT

Before you can write fascinating articles, you have to build up your writing "muscles." Just as an athlete lifts weights or a musician practices scales, you must train regularly. You cannot wait until you are in the mood or feel inspired. Once you have some hefty writing muscles, you will be ready to start working on your first article.

Tips and techniques
Set a regular amount of time and a schedule for your writing. It could be 10 minutes every morning before breakfast or one hour twice a week after supper. Then, come rain or shine, stick to your schedule.

Now it's your turn

Unlock your ideas

Begin your writing practice with some timed brainstorming. Go to your writing place. Close your eyes for a minute and relax. Think about things you have heard about in the news or an interesting story that someone told you. Let your mind wander over everything you've seen, heard, and done recently. Think about things that interest you and topics you'd like to know more about. Now open your eyes and write "Story Ideas" on a piece of paper. Start scribbling! Give yourself five minutes to write as many ideas as you can think of. Now stop. You are on your way to writing an article.

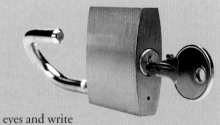

Now it's your turn

Make the real-life connection
Look over your list from the last exercise. Pick your five favorite ideas from the list. Maybe you wrote down dogs. Or travel. Or scuba diving. Now take 10 minutes to write a short paragraph about each one. What is interesting about each idea? Why do you want to write about it? What do you hope to learn? What would you want to tell readers about that topic? Write your ideas without worrying about correct punctuation or writing in complete sentences. Just let your ideas flow. When you are finished, read all five paragraphs again. Circle the one that interests you the most. You just may have found the subject of your article.

CASE STUDY

When it's time to come up with a list of story ideas, writer Meg Moss and her magazine co-workers head to the library. "We get a room, pull out a bunch of books and have a brainstorming session," she says. "One of the best ways to generate ideas is to sit down and talk with people."

STORY DEVELOPMENT	WINNING WORDS	SCINTILLATING SPEECH	HINTS AND TIPS	THE NEXT STEP

TWO SIDES TO EVERY STORY

Today most newspapers and magazines strive for objectivity. That means that they try to tell all sides of every story. They want stories to be based on facts, not the personal opinions and beliefs of their writers or editors.

But that hasn't always been the case. Long ago, some newspapers existed solely to give the opinions of writers and editors. The first newspaper in the American colonies, for example, was *The New-England Courant*. It was published by Benjamin Franklin's brother, James, to promote his political opinions. It did not have balanced articles.

The New York Times, which was founded in 1851, made balanced reporting about issues an important principle in newspaper publishing. Balanced reporting means that a writer includes information, quotes, and viewpoints from all sides of a story. It is important to keep that in mind as you plan and research your article.

Now it's your turn

Turn the tables

Write the subject of your article on a blank sheet of paper. Give yourself a few minutes to think about all the people, places, or things that are connected to your subject. Now write "Positive" on one side of the paper. Write everything that is improved or that is good underneath it. On the other side, write "Negative." Write everything that is made worse or that is bad underneath it. Keep both lists in mind while you are researching and writing your article. Find people who can talk about both sides, if you can, and try to write an article that balances all sides.

Voicing an opinion

Personal opinions have a place in modern journalism. Most newspapers have designated opinion pages where writers can take a stand on issues. Newspapers also run editorials, which usually present an opinion supported by the majority of the paper's editorial board. The board usually consists of the publisher, the editorial page editor, and editorial writers, but not reporters. Editorials and opinion articles are always separated from other articles. That way, readers know they express opinions and are not unbiased news stories.

Some television and radio journalists also voice their opinions. TV and radio news programs are often hosted by people who have clearly stated beliefs. They interview guests who might agree or disagree with their opinions. This leads to spirited debates that entertain viewers and listeners. The shows may help people form their own opinions.

The Internet also offers writers an opportunity to be opinionated. There are many Web logs, called blogs, that contain personal opinions about various subjects or events in the news. Readers are often invited to add their own opinions and thoughts about a blogger's commentary.

FIND YOUR VOICE

Reading books and newspaper, magazine, and online articles will help you discover your own style of writing—your writer's voice.

Every good writer has a style of writing that is unique to that person. It takes lots of practice to acquire this unique voice. Writers continue to develop their voices throughout their lives.

Finding your writer's voice

Once you start reading as a writer, you will notice how writers have their own rhythm, style, and range of language that stay the same throughout their work. News articles are usually solid and straightforward, but the information in feature articles is presented in each writer's style. Learning to recognize the different techniques writers use to craft their articles is like learning to identify different kinds of music.

Experiment

The best way to recognize style is to read articles by several writers. Look at several newspapers and magazines. In each one, pick one piece to read. Study that article for style and voice. How are the articles different? Do you like the more straightforward approach used in newspaper articles? Or do you prefer the more conversational tone often used in magazine articles?

CASE STUDY

Joe Grimm, a longtime journalist at the Detroit *Free Press*, encourages young writers to read as much as they can. That includes newspapers, magazines, and books. "People who do not read print journalism are not likely to work in it," he says. "Good writing will be the raw material of your own good writing."

Writers' voices

Look at the kinds of words these two writers use. Do they use lots of adjectives? What about the length and rhythm of their sentences? Which style do you prefer to read?

Peg Lopata

A tiny white ball as light as popcorn flies faster than the eye can see, over a table measuring just five by nine feet. Players slice, swipe, and smash at a ball weighing less than an ounce. The audience gasps, oooohs, and bursts into applause, all eyes glued to the action. The ball skims the table, the player rears back to return it—but it curves and spins away from his flailing paddle. The game is over. The loser faces a disappointed coach; the winner, the adoring crowd. And you've just experienced a small taste of China's very popular sport: Ping-Pong.
Peg Lopata, "Paddle Power," *Faces,* May 2007

Meg Moss

What's the first thing you do in a dark room? Turn on the light, of course. Going outside after dinner? Grab a flashlight. You probably don't even think about the falling darkness as day slips quietly into night. Lights twinkle on and life continues.
 Imagine what life was like before you could flip a switch. For most of history, with no electricity to light up cities, streets, or living rooms, the nighttime was truly dark. Until Thomas Edison invented the electric lightbulb—100 times brighter than a candle—people depended on fire. They burned wood, oil, or gas in torches, fireplaces, and primitive lamps. Stinky but cheap candles made of animal fat dimly lit many homes.
Meg Moss, "Summer, Winter, Spring, Fall … Night?"
Ask, October 2007

JUST THE FACTS

Before you begin to write your article, you should make sure that you have all the facts you need.

One way to do that is to create an outline. This will help you focus on what information is most important to the topic of your article. It will also help you recognize what areas you should research further.

Often you can find important information in other articles or books that have been written about the subjects you are writing about.

The Internet is another good place to look for facts. Be wary of Internet sources, though. Not all of them are reliable. Often, the best way to get firsthand information for a story is to interview the people who are involved in it.

CASE STUDY

During his research, California writer Brad Herzog often reads many articles on the subject he's writing about. Sometimes the facts in those articles are reported differently. Noticing all of those differences helps him prepare questions for his interviews. He makes a list of everything he's read and then asks the people he talks to which facts are correct.

Five W's and an H

In journalism, the five W's and an H represent the essential elements that must be included in every news article, whether it is for a newspaper, magazine, or Web site.

Who: This is the people involved. It can include the subject of the article and people who are affected by the subject matter.

What: This is the action taking place. It tells what the "who" in your story is doing.

When: This is the time element. It tells when the action is taking place.

Where: This is the place where the action is happening.

Why: This explains the action. It tells why it happens, why it is important, and why people should care.

How: This describes the way the action occurs.

Now it's your turn

Look for holes

Write the subject of your article at the top of a sheet of paper. Underneath it, write down the five W's and an H: Who, What, When, Where, Why, How. Under each word, write down all the details you know about it. Once you have this list filled out, you will know if there are any holes in your reporting and what other facts you should try to find out.

FACTS COME TO LIFE

Facts are the backbone of any article you write. But facts can sometimes be dry and boring. They need your writing and reporting skills to bring them to life.

Think about the story behind the facts, the interesting details that will make the article more enjoyable to read. To get those details, you must be observant when interviewing people and doing your research. You should notice all of the many small details. Then you will have to find fresh ways to write about them.

Tips and techniques

Be accurate. Journalists may be sued for libel if they knowingly write false statements that damage someone's reputation. They will also damage their own credibility and the credibility of the publication for which they are writing.

Now it's your turn

Add the spice of life

Look for details to include in your article. Often this will help facts seem more interesting.

- If you are writing about an event that is taking place, get there early to see what happens beforehand. Are people waiting for it to start? Is it being set up at the last minute? Are there decorations? If so, what are they like? What kind of music is playing?

- If you are writing about a person, notice everything you can about him or her. What kind of clothes is he wearing? Does he stroke his beard while he talks? Does she check her watch or look out the window? Is the interview interrupted by a phone call or a visitor?

- If you are writing about a subject like an animal or a sporting event, uncover every interesting and quirky detail that you can. How much does the animal weigh, and how does that compare with how much the average sixth-grader weighs? When was the game first played, and who played it? What did the uniforms look like?

Remember, not every detail you write down will be important to your article. But some of them will help make the story more interesting and fun to read.

CASE STUDY

Facts can be fun. In a magazine story about night, for example, Meg Moss included some amazing statistics that are fun to read. "Night is huge," she wrote. "It covers 98.5 million square miles of the Earth's surface all the time."

STORY DEVELOPMENT	WINNING WORDS	SCINTILLATING SPEECH	HINTS AND TIPS	THE NEXT STEP

BE A REPORTER

Some people think of reporters as pushy and rude. They picture them surrounding people, thrusting microphones into faces, and shouting questions. Sometimes that is what reporters do. But most reporters are polite.

Reporters know that to get a good story, they have to ask thoughtful questions. They know they have to be good listeners. Sometimes it can be hard to be a reporter. Sometimes you have to ask embarassing or painful questions. But if you are kind and respectful, you will often get good answers.

When Paula Murphey wrote about a tornado that struck a small town in Alabama for *Boys' Life* magazine, she had to talk to kids who had witnessed the storm and who had lost friends or family members. It isn't easy to talk to people about such sad things. But Murphey was able to get good answers:

"Our friends needed us," Chris Czarnecki says. *"We felt we should do anything possible to help."*

Scout Conner Richey, 13, was near the high school when the tornado passed about 30 yards in front of his family's car, nearly picking it up. He watched the twister hit the school, where one of his best friends was killed. "Through all of this, I've learned how people can come together," he says.

"I was shell-shocked from what happened," Remington Mollett says. "But after a week of funerals, I really wanted to keep doing all I could to help."

Paula Murphey, "Our Friends Needed Us," *Boys' Life*, August 2007

Now it's your turn

Be prepared

Write the name of the person you are interviewing on a sheet of paper. Then write down a list of questions you want to ask that person. It will help if you have already found out a little bit about this person. You can look for other articles about him or her, or look on the Internet for information. Having background information will help you come up with good questions to ask. It will also save you time during the interview. "You don't want to waste time asking questions that you could have gotten answered from doing your research," Brad Herzog says. "Don't ask them where they were born, because you should be able to find that out. Instead, ask them what it was like growing up there."

Tips and techniques

Use a tape recorder, take notes, or do both during interviews. That will help you record the most complete and accurate information possible. Not everyone is comfortable being recorded, so be certain to ask about this at the beginning of the interview. Bring new batteries, a spare tape, and an extra pen along with you, just in case you need them.

Tips and techniques

Always make an appointment to speak with a source in person. If you are calling someone on the phone, ask if he or she has time to talk now or if there would be a better time to call back.

CASE STUDY

Before Jacqui Banaszynski leaves the office for an interview, she talks to her editor or to another reporter about what questions she should be sure to ask. Then she writes a little list of topics at the top of her notebook. "That helps me prioritize my time in the interview," she says.

TIME TO TALK

It might not feel natural the first time you interview someone. Even reporters who have been interviewing people for years struggle with it.

"It's still not easy for me," Jacqui Banaszynski says. "The only reason I've been able to get through it is because my curiosity and my desire to learn is greater than my self-consciousness about the process." If you're nervous, the best thing you can do is to act naturally. Be polite. Speak slowly and clearly. Introduce yourself and tell your source what you are writing about. And try to look your subject in the eye as much as you can.

Tips and techniques
Leave the door open for follow-up questions. Ask your subject if you can call him or her if you have additional questions or need more information. Be sure to get a phone number.

CASE STUDY
When Jacqui Banaszynski gets nervous about an interview, she reminds herself that it isn't about her. "I put a conscious focus on the person I'm interviewing and pay all of my attention to asking the right questions and to getting it all in my notebook. If you keep the focus off yourself, life gets a lot easier."

Now it's your turn

First things first

Bring a list of questions with you to the interview. The first question on the list should always be, "How do you spell your name?" After you have that detail taken care of, ask a few easy questions. That will help relax both you and your subject. Try to ask questions that are open-ended, not yes or no questions. You will get longer answers and have more to write about. Here are some examples to consider:

• How did that make you feel?
• Why do you think that happened?
• What did you do next?
• What are your plans?
• How will you make that happen?

Tips and techniques

Dress appropriately for your interview. Consider what your source will be wearing. If you are talking to a government official, wear nice clothes. If you are talking to a playground supervisor at an elementary school, jeans and a sweatshirt are OK.

CASE STUDY

"The best reporters engage their interviewees and put them at ease," says Lynn Closway, a longtime newspaper and magazine writer. She remembers watching a reporter talk to a doctor who was nervous. They had a casual chat first, which calmed the doctor. "The doctor could hardly tell when the casual banter ended and the real interview began," Closway says. "It was a more believable, less-rehearsed, sincere interview."

STORY DEVELOPMENT	WINNING WORDS	SCINTILLATING SPEECH	HINTS AND TIPS	THE NEXT STEP

INTERESTING SUBJECTS

The subjects of a news article or feature article are not like characters in a novel or a short story. Usually those characters are made up out of the writer's imagination.

The subjects in news or feature articles are never made up. They are real people. Maybe they are super bike riders. Or maybe they win trivia contests. Or maybe they are soccer phenoms. They are often just as interesting as make-believe people.

Paint a picture

Your words can show readers what a person looks like. They can tell readers how that person acts, talks, and even smells. They can help readers understand more about a person.

But because newspaper and magazine articles aren't as long as books, you have to give those details quickly. You have to choose your words carefully. Instead of saying that someone is strong, show how that person is strong, as in this example from a *Sports Illustrated Kids* article about Minnesota Vikings football player Adrian Peterson:

> *At age two, he could support his weight while hanging by his arms from a door. By eight, he was dizzying youth football defenses with his speed.*
> Sean Jensen, "Runaway Success," *Sports Illustrated Kids*, Winter 2007

Tips and techniques

Talk to your sources in person whenever possible. People sometimes communicate with their faces and their bodies more than with their words. You will learn much more about the people you are writing about if you are able to meet them.

Now it's your turn

Adjectives are important

Write your subject's name on a piece of paper. Then give yourself five minutes to write down all the adjectives you can think of to describe that person. Include both physical descriptions, such as "tall," "tan," or "muscular," and character descriptions, such as "quiet," "thoughtful," or "silly." Write down every word that comes to mind when you think of that person. You will not use all of these adjectives in your article. But if you choose the ones that seem most relevant to your subject matter, you will help bring the story and the people in it to life.

The opening paragraph of a profile about actor David Henrie in *Girls' Life Magazine* describes what it was like to interview him that particular day, which helps describe what he is like in general:

> *David had come down with a bout of pneumonia the day we met him, but trooper that he is, he came out of his trailer to chat with* Girls' Life *for quite a bit. Even under the weather, he won us over. We wanted to spoonfeed him medicine and make the little darlin' feel all better.*
> Kelly White, "Triple Threat,"
> *Girls' Life Magazine,*
> February/March 2008

Tips and techniques

Read as many articles about the people you are interviewing as possible. Not only will you learn more about those people, you might also get ideas of other people to interview.

WRITE IN 3-D

Look at a photograph of yourself. Even if it is a great picture, it only shows one side of you. It is flat. That's because cameras cannot capture a person in 3-D.

In writing, you can make your characters round. They will seem much more lifelike to readers if you show all sides of them. That doesn't mean you have to focus on negative qualities about people. Writing about challenges they have faced or problems they have had— and how they handled them—will make them more interesting. When you do write about a person who has negative attributes, don't avoid including those. Remember, you need to tell both sides of the story.

Tips and techniques

When writing a profile, ask your subject to recommend some other sources for you to contact. Those sources could be that person's family members, friends, or co-workers.

CASE STUDY

Brad Herzog graduated from the same college as Dr. Henry Heimlich (right), who invented the Heimlich maneuver, which is used to help people who are choking. When he wrote a profile of Heimlich for the Cornell University magazine, he talked to Heimlich. He also talked to many other people about the doctor. He found out that some people didn't like Heimlich and that he had controversial beliefs. Having different perspectives about Heimlich helped Herzog write a much better story. All of that research helped him win an award for his article.

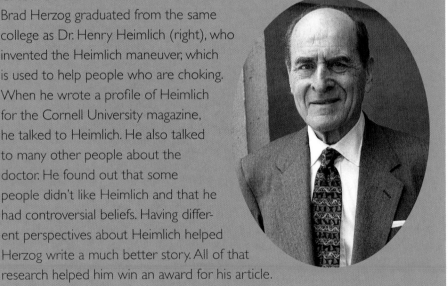

| GETTING STARTED | GETTING THE STORY | PEOPLE | VIEWPOINT |

Relying on others

Occasionally the subjects of your stories—the people you most want to talk to—can't be interviewed. Perhaps they are no longer alive. Perhaps they are unable to communicate. Or perhaps they just don't want to talk to a writer. That doesn't mean you can't write about them. You just have to work harder. You have to find other people who can tell you about them. You will probably have to do many more interviews to get the whole story. But it is still possible to do it.

When Meg Moss writes about people, it is often about people who lived long ago. She has to write about them using historical information and the words of other people. To write about the castaways in an article for a children's magazine, she used writings from people who had been involved in a shipwreck in 1760.

Blown off course on the way to its dark chore, Utile *wrecked on the dangerous reefs around a tiny and remote coral island. About 70 slaves, trapped behind hatches nailed shut, drowned in the shipwreck. Twenty French crew members died as well. The rest swam through beating surf and blustering wind to the relative safety of the island.*

In the coming weeks 20 more slaves died, as the ship's crew hoarded the small freshwater supply. The sailors constructed a raft from the wreckage and escaped the island, leaving supplies enough for three months and promising to send help. When they told their story in Mauritius, however, the governor refused to rescue the remaining castaways.

So, on that treeless, windblown sandbank less than a mile square, the stranded slaves struggled— for 15 years!—to survive. By the time Captain Tromelin of the sailing ship La Dauphine *found them in November 1776, only seven women and a baby boy were left. The women reported having kept the same fire burning throughout the years.*
Meg Moss, "Survivors," *Muse,* September 2007

PERSONALITY PROFILES

Personality profiles are often included in many newspapers and magazines. Profiles are a little bit like biographies, except they are much shorter and far less detailed.

Sometimes a profile is written because someone has done something special. Maybe a firefighter saved a life. Possibly a teacher won a big award. Sometimes it commemorates an important event. Sometimes it tells about a well-known person, such as an athlete or a celebrity. Sometimes profiles are written just because a person is interesting.

Sports Illustrated Kids profiled Indianapolis Colts quarterback Peyton Manning (left) because he was selected as the Athlete of the Year in 2007:

Yes Manning was an awesome passer. He had more touchdown passes, completions, and yards in his first eight NFL seasons than any other QB at the start of his career. Yes he had transformed the Colts into reliable winners ... Yes Manning was living a pretty charmed life, marrying his college sweetheart, making funny TV commercials, and earning millions of dollars.

But that big mark was always there: Peyton Manning had never led his team to a Super Bowl Championship.

Last February, on a rainy night in Miami, that mark became history.
Ted Keith, "Peyton Is Your #1," *Sports Illustrated Kids*, December 2007

Faces, a world cultures magazine for kids, includes profiles about young people from various places around the world. Often, kids write those profiles. Abby Hackl, a 12-year-old who visited Tunisia, wrote a profile about a boy named Ghassen Chakroun:

Ghassen is a Muslim and attends a nearby mosque. He prays at least five times each day. Prayer times are announced from the mosque. Each prayer involves counted verses. The thing that Ghassen would most like for Americans to know about Islam is that it prohibits doing bad things, harming or insulting others. ...

If Ghassen could show an American child his country, he would also like to show them the beautiful city of Aindrahem and share tasty Tunisian food with them. Native dishes include couscous, saffron potatoes, coucha (a slow-baked lamb dish flavored with olive oil, mint, cayenne pepper and turmeric), and tuna with cucumbers. Ghassen loves his country and is proud of its traditions and culture.
Abby Christine Hackl, "Life in Tunisia," *Faces*, February 2008

STAYING OUT OF THE STORY

Most news stories are told from an objective point of view. The person writing the article is not involved in the article.

The writer reports facts, as well as other people's feelings, thoughts, and opinions. But the writer's own feelings, thoughts, and opinions should not be apparent in the article. Even in a news article, however, the writer has choices about how to tell the story.

From the facts

Some articles are based primarily on facts. These articles are meant to inform readers about a particular subject. The writer's job is to study the facts, then present them in a clear and interesting way. Meg Moss often writes fact-based stories for *Ask*, an arts and science magazine. She works hard to make the facts fun in her articles, as in this part of a story about volcanoes:

Volcanoes come in many sizes. To describe volcanoes, scientists use words such as gentle, explosive, large, severe, colossal, supercolossal, and—no kidding—humongous. This scale is based on a volcano's explosivity, that is, how much ash, rock, and gas it hurls out and how high the eruption cloud, or plume, jets into the air.
Meg Moss, "Volcanoes Rock the World," *Ask*, October 2005

| GETTING STARTED | GETTING THE STORY | PEOPLE | VIEWPOINT |

He said, she said

Some articles are told with the help of other people. Quotes from various sources are used to tell a story and inform readers about a particular subject. The writer's job is to gather those quotes and combine them with facts to tell a story. Quotes can make a story more credible and conversational. They allow readers to hear someone's actual words about a subject.

For her story about a tornado in *Boys' Life* magazine, Paula Murphey interviewed several Boy Scouts who had experienced the storm. She interspersed their statements with descriptions of the event and facts about what happened:

The damage included the meeting building for Troop 21, Americus, Ga., where a fallen tree took off part of its roof and knocked down a wall. Destruction was everywhere in town.

"The tornado went right through my dad's business, destroying it," says Life Scout Theo Baldwin, 17. All around there were "trees through brick walls, collapsed ceilings, big steel I-beams bent."

"A tornado hit my friends' houses about 200 yards from my house," says Life Scout Will Meadows, 14. "They have to move out and are having to rebuild."

Here, as in Alabama, local Scouts rose to the occasion. In Americus, troops cleared rubble around town and pitched in at the Red Cross headquarters, helping unload, inventory and organize relief supplies and equipment.

"We also distributed water to needy people [affected] by the tornado," Will says. "It was scary hearing their stories of how they barely escaped."

Paula Murphey, "Our Friends Needed Us," *Boys' Life*, August 2007

OTHER POINTS OF VIEW

There are times when newspaper and magazine writers can write from other points of view.

The first-person viewpoint allows the writer to be part of the story and to refer to himself or herself as "I." In these cases, your own observations and opinions are an important part of the story. But that is only appropriate in certain kinds of writing.

Columns

Many newspapers and magazines carry columns written in the first-person point of view. Columns are not news articles. Sometimes they are about funny subjects. Sometimes they are about a writer's area of expertise, such as technology or cooking. Sometimes they are about events in the news. The writer analyzes the news and gives an opinion about it. Columns are usually separated from news articles. Sometimes the writer's picture is placed next to the column.

Every issue of *Discovery Girls*, for example, includes a column written by the publisher of the magazine. She tells readers a story that relates to that particular issue. Here's one about her friends in middle school:

When I was in middle school, I hung out with these three girls, and we did a lot of things together. But my parents didn't like for me to have more than two friends sleep over at one time.

That was really hard on me, because it meant I had to leave out one of my friends. One weekend, I invited over two of my friends and left out one, Shelly. The worst part was that I didn't even tell Shelly myself that she couldn't spend the night. I was going to ... but my other friends told her first.

Catherine Lee, "Catherine's Page," *Discovery Girls*, February/March 2008

Reviews

Many people rely on reviews to pick which movies they will watch or what books they will read. They make their decisions based in part on the opinions of the person who writes the review. That's why reviewers sometimes include first-person comments along with facts and descriptions in their articles. Reviewers are expected to describe the movie or book, critically evaluate it, and tell what someone would or wouldn't like about it. To do that, they often give their own impressions and opinions.

In his review of the book *Shanghai Messenger* in *Faces* magazine, Alex Wells used the first-person voice to explain what the story meant to him.

I learned about China, its people and everyday life from this book. Shanghai Messenger was interesting to read because it was written in poetic form. The words fit with the setting because they sounded Chinese. Shanghai Messenger was both fascinating and informative.
Alex Wells, "Guest Review: *Shanghai Messenger,*" *Faces*, May 2007

Personal stories

Some stories are told best in the voice of the writer. When a writer experiences something unique, writing about it in first person allows him or her to share what happened in a more personal way. Often those personal experiences are combined with facts and quotes to tell a more complete story.

In *American Girl* magazine, a young girl named Alex wrote a first-person article about surviving cancer. Because she told it from her own point of view, the story is both more personal and powerful.

A big side effect of chemo is that you lose your hair. I was really hoping that it wouldn't happen to me, but it did. Big clumps of hair started coming out as I brushed, and eventually I was completely bald. I got lots of hats and a wig. I wore the wig on special occasions when I didn't want people to see that I was bald. The wig was itchy, though, and I didn't like wearing it. I mostly stuck to hats, and I got used to having no hair. Even my eyebrows and eyelashes fell out. It was weird.
Alex (last name withheld), "Alex's Story," *American Girl*, April 2008

MAKE A STRONG START

The first paragraph of your article is the most important paragraph you will write. It is called the lead.

The lead has to draw readers in. It has to tell them what the story is about. It has to tell them why the story is important. It has to make them want to read the article. And it has to do all of that quickly. Some editors suggest that leads be no more than 30 words long. That means you have to pick the best words and ideas to use in your lead.

Good ways to lead

There are many ways to approach a lead. You have to decide which way works best for your story. That will depend on what kind of story you are writing and where it will be published. News articles need to get to the point quickly, but the leads in magazine features can be longer. Reading leads from other articles will help you think of ideas for your own lead.

News leads summarize the story. They focus on the facts. Articles in newspapers and news magazines often have news leads.

On February 26, a bank on an island in the Arctic opened its doors. It accepted its first deposit, which was a container of rice seeds from 104 countries. One day, the Svalbard Global Seed Vault will hold the seeds of every crop on the planet.
Martha Pickerill, editor, "The Farmers' Bank," *Time for Kids*, March 7, 2008

Description leads set the scene of a story. They show a picture of someone or something that is important to the story.

One look at the walls of Steve Zainer's office in Milwaukee, Wisconsin, will have you nodding in amazement. Zainer has more than 800 bobbleheads, or as insiders call them, nodders.
Sarah Braunstein, "Ultimate Sports Collections," *Sports Illustrated Kids*, December 2007

Question leads ask readers about their interest in the story. They tell readers that the answers to the question will be in the article. They can be used for most kinds of articles.

Would you like to understand your dog's dialogue? How about your cat's chitchat? It's easy. Just use your eyes.
Ruth Musgrave, "Decoding DogSpeak," *National Geographic Kids*, March 2006

STAY FOCUSED

For some writers, the lead is the hardest part of an article to write.

Sometimes writing the lead takes as long as, or longer than, writing the rest of the article. The lead sets the tone for the rest of the story. It gives the article direction. The lead has a lot of work to do. But it must also be simple. It should be concise. It should stay focused on the primary idea of the article. Keep the purpose of your article in mind while you work on your lead.

An interesting quote in the lead can reveal something essential about the article.

"Great God! This is an awful place ... ," said British explorer Sir Robert Falcon Scott of Antarctica in 1912. He had no idea that the world's coldest and windiest continent would become one of the best places in the world for scientists to study the Earth. Christine Graf, "Science in a Land of Extremes," *Faces,* May 2006

Imaginative leads quickly draw the reader into the article.

If Earth had a belly button, it would be the Tibetan Plateau in Central Asia. Framed by the Kunlun Mountains to the north and the Himalayan Mountains to the south, the Earth here seems to poke out. Dan Risch, "Life at the Top," *Faces,* May 2006

Tips and techniques

Keep your sentences short. Try reading each one out loud. If you have to take a breath before you finish a sentence, it's too long.

Now it's your turn

Thinking ahead

It's a good idea to be thinking about what you want to say in your lead the whole time you are researching the article. When you are ready to start writing, you will be ready to put your thoughts into words. Take a few minutes to look through your notes and research. Are there any good quotes that set up the story? Did you find a great anecdote about your subject? Do you have any fascinating facts that you could string together for the lead? Should the article be explained with a straightforward, summary lead? Try writing a few leads. Have a friend, parent, or teacher read each one. Ask which one gives the best idea of what the story is about. Which one is the easiest to read? Which one makes the reader want to read more?

Anecdote leads tell a story. They introduce characters who play a role in the rest of the article, and they set the scene. Sometimes good anecdote leads take a few sentences.

On a bitterly cold night in January 1789, James Madison suffered a frostbitten nose. It happened while he was campaigning in his Virginia district for the House of Representatives of the first Congress of the United States. Madison and his opponent, James Monroe, had stood outside a church to publicly debate the issues of the campaign. By the time Madison had finished his long ride home afterward, his nose was frozen. Virginia Calkins, "Give the People What They Want," *Cobblestone*, December 2007

MORE TO THE STORY

Now that you have your readers' attention, you have to give them the rest of the story.

The first step in that process is to tell them why you are writing the article and what it means to them. There are many ways to do this. You can use a quote from an important person. You can use facts from your research. You can use your own writing to summarize the story. The important thing is that you do it early in the article.

In a nutshell

The lead sets up the story and draws the readers in. The next paragraph should tell them why the story is being written. It sums up the reason for the story in a nutshell. That's why some writers call it a "nut graf." A nut graf (short for paragraph) is especially important in feature stories, when the lead might not give the point of the story.

Paula Murphey's lead about the Alabama tornadoes introduced some of the people who were involved and set the scene for the devastation to come. Her nut graf, then, creates context for the rest of the article:

CASE STUDY

"Nut grafs are like secret decoder rings," Jacqui Banaszynski says. "They tell the reader, here's what I'm going to be telling you and here's why I'm telling it to you."

> *The Enterprise tornado was part of a storm system that barreled through the Midwest and South on March 1, spawning tornadoes that left 20 people dead in three states. Among the victims were friends and a family member of the Scouts in Enterprise.*
> Paula Murphey, "Our Friends Needed Us," *Boys' Life*, August 2007

Now it's your turn

Put it in a sentence

Try writing your own nut graf. Write one sentence that sums up the purpose of your article. Focus just on the facts; don't use adjectives, quotes, or other details. When you feel as though you have crafted a sentence that quickly and clearly summarizes your article, tack it up on your bulletin board or put it in a prominent place on your desk. You should refer to that sentence while you are writing your article. It will remind you exactly what you are writing about.

Keep it moving

The body of the article should support both the lead and the nut graf. It should include the rest of the important information you have gathered about the subject. Sometimes newspaper and magazine writers can do that in

300 or 400 words. Sometimes it takes 2,000 words or more. The length of the article is not what matters most. It is most important to tell all the essential details. You should continue writing until the story has been told to completion.

Inverted pyramid

You already know what a pyramid is. It has a small point at the top but a wide bottom. When you invert a pyramid, you turn it upside down. The wide part is at the top, and the small point is at the bottom. Many newspaper writers use the inverted pyramid as a guideline for writing articles. The most interesting and important information is given first, in the lead. The information that follows gets less and less important. The least important details come at the end. That is especially important if your news article has to be trimmed. Sometimes articles are too long for the space allotted, and sentences must be cut. So don't put important information at the end.

Not all articles follow the inverted pyramid format. Feature articles can be written with delayed leads, which work up to the most important parts—kind of like the punch line of a joke.

CHAPTER 6: WINNING WORDS

MAKE YOUR WORDS WORK

Words are the heart of your article. They can bring the story to life, or they can let it die weakly right in front of the reader's eyes. It is up to you to choose strong action words that will keep your article humming along.

Tight and bright

Your goal as an article writer should be to write tightly and brightly. Don't use five average words to describe something or someone. One strong, descriptive word can have a much greater impact on the reader. Choose strong, bold verbs and concise nouns. Lots of adjectives and long sentences will slow readers down. Notice how Sean McCollum carefully selected the words he used in a story about a group of Boy Scouts who spent the night in the notorious prison Alcatraz:

> *As night fell and the boys unrolled their sleeping bags, Alcatraz revealed its quieter side. Mice skittered across the floor above. The sound of wind and surf rose and fell beyond the walls. The scent of the bay drifted indoors.*
> Sean McCollum, "Escape to Alcatraz," *Boys' Life*, October 2007

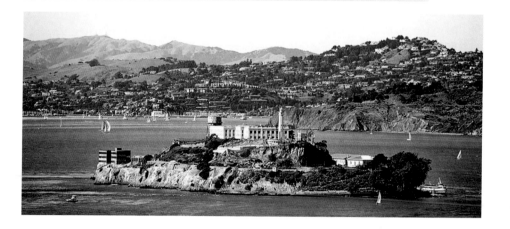

| GETTING STARTED | | GETTING THE STORY | PEOPLE | VIEWPOINT |

Tips and techniques

Bring scenes to life with vivid word pictures called metaphors and similes. A metaphor describes something by calling it something else—"Her eyes were blue oceans," for example. A simile describes something by comparing it with something else with the word like or as. For example, "She's as fresh as a daisy."

Now it's your turn

Lively words

Make a list of 10 everyday action words. Then have fun brainstorming at least four substitutes for each word. Perhaps someone would "mastermind" instead of "plan," or something would "smack" instead of "hit." Use a thesaurus for extra help. Make every word count.

CASE STUDY

Choosing the right words is part of the fun for Meg Moss. She enjoyed trying to coming up with a fun name for a clam that was reportedly the oldest living animal on Earth. "I was thinking about something like 'Senior Shellfish' or something like that," she says. "It's like music or poetry, I think. You choose words that sound nice and feel good."

Tips and techniques

Avoid the word "very." It is very overused (sorry!) and doesn't say much. Instead pick a word that says it all: "ecstatic" instead of "very excited," or "stunning" instead of "very pretty."

SHOW, DON'T TELL

Let your words create a vivid image of your subject matter. Write about the specific details so readers can see what you are writing about. Show them exactly what it looks, sounds, or even smells like.

Be an active writer

Engage all of your senses as a writer. If you're writing about a farm, be sure to mention the pungent aroma of manure. If you're writing about the school cafeteria, describe how the food looks, smells, and tastes (but be sure to avoid purely personal opinion).

If you're writing about a baseball game, tell readers what a home run sounds like. Can you hear the ball hit the bat? Does the crowd cheer? Does the pitcher groan in disgust? Describe those details in your article.

Here's how Meg Moss used strong action words in a story about locusts:

Day and night, their chewing and chomping sounded like a huge herd of grazing cattle. The locusts scrambled over each other in a feeding frenzy and piled up inches deep all around. They crunched underfoot and clung to clothing. Train tracks became so slimy with locust bodies that locomotives slid dangerously.
Meg Moss, "Swarm!" *Ask*, May/June 2005

Tips and techniques
Some interesting tidbits of information or important facts and figures may not fit smoothly within your article. Separate these nuggets into sidebars, which are short pieces of separate text (like this one).

CASE STUDY

Jacqui Banaszynski encourages writers to think of their writing as a painting hanging in an art museum. The people looking at it should be able to tell what it is immediately. "You don't want them squinting at your master-piece, wondering if it's someone's vague notion of fruit," she says. "You want them to know—

bam!—it's a Granny Smith apple with a small blemish just under the stem. This is how you make your readers see what you saw." Using specific details, she says, keeps stories fresh. It also improves your skills as a writer and reporter. "Looking for specific details makes you a sharper reporter," she says. "Choosing which details are relevant makes you a crisper writer."

Tips and techniques
Use only one idea per sentence. Don't try to tell every fact or relevant detail at once. Split up sentences and paragraphs so each one is easy to read and to understand. Spread your details throughout the article.

Tips and techniques
Use subheads at the start of different sections in your article. Subheads are like mini-titles that tell what the focus of that section will be. They help break up the story and make it easier to read.

LESS IS MORE

In news articles, more is not necessarily better. But writing less is not necessarily easier.

Unlike authors, who can devote entire chapters to certain subjects, news writers have to pack a lot of information into a few words. You have to recognize what information is important and what isn't. You have to decide what facts can be included and what details aren't needed. Sometimes you have to leave funny quotes or cute stories out of an article.

Leave them out

One of the commandments of journalistic writing is to omit unnecessary words. If a word does not add something to the story, delete it. Avoid phrases that waste words; instead of saying "the reason why is that," simply use "because." Not only will it give you more room to write about more important matters, it will also make your article easier to read.

The articles in *Time for Kids* are only a few paragraphs long. The writers have to work hard to tell the important information and make it interesting to read.

The New York Philharmonic played a historic concert in Pyongyang, North Korea, on February 26. It was the first time a major cultural group from the U.S. had performed in North Korea. The two countries do not get along. The U.S. and other nations want North Korea to end its illegal program to create deadly weapons.

"Through our music, we will be able to express our friendly feelings to the North Korean people," said Lorin Maazel, music director of the New York Philharmonic. After the concert, people stood and clapped for five minutes. Martha Pickerill, editor, "The Power of Music," *Time for Kids*, March 7, 2008

CASE STUDY

It can be harder to write a short story than a long one, Lynn Closway says. "Writing a short story takes organization and self-editing," she says. "Write your piece, then take a critical look at it, get out the scalpel and cut out anything that may seem extra."

Cut your darlings

The fact that you like the way a sentence sounds or you think a quote is funny doesn't mean it belongs in your article. Sometimes you have to cut out your favorite parts of a story to make it work. Stay focused on relevant details and important facts.

Now it's your turn

Listen carefully

Read through every draft of your article out loud. Notice sentences that are too long or places where details pile up. Notice areas that might confuse readers. Use a red pen or colored highlighter to mark any areas that seem too wordy or don't fit with the rest of the article. Then go back and eliminate as many of those extra words as you can.

IN THEIR OWN WORDS

Unlike writers of fiction, article writers do not make up sentences and put them in the mouths of their subjects. Instead, they use quotes—the exact words that were spoken by other people.

You will be the writer of your article, but you will also rely on the words of others. Most news articles and magazine features include quotes from the people involved. Every quote you write must use exactly the same words that were spoken by your source. Quotes are a great way to give readers a sense of someone's personality while passing along information at the same time.

Quality quotations

Quotes can help illustrate facts. They can prove points, offer insight, or tell a secret. The best quotes are short and sweet. Sometimes they are also funny. They should always add something interesting to an article. Don't use quotes that repeat information you've already written. Make sure they say something new in an interesting way.

In this example, a short quote from football player Antonio Gates, the subject of a profile in *Sports Illustrated Kids,* adds emphasis to the information the writer has already provided:

> *At the start of his career, Gates's long layoff from football was seen as a negative. But Gates thinks it might have been a blessing. In college football a star player's athleticism can make up for sloppy route running or poor blocking technique. Gates didn't have any bad habits when he arrived at his first [San Diego] Chargers training camp. In fact, he says, "I didn't have any habits."*
>
> Gary Gramling, "In Good Hands," *Sports Illustrated Kids,* December 2007

An excerpt from an article about jack-o'-lanterns shows how the writer combined quotes with the description of how to carve a pumpkin. The quotes add personality to the article:

"Carved pumpkins with triangle eyes are far too common," Farmer Mike [Valladao] says. *"If you want a really cool Halloween pumpkin, it needs character. My style is called Pumpkin Carving in the Round."*

Instead of punching holes in the pumpkin, Valladao (right) used the rind to create an illusion of depth. This method can be used on any pumpkin but is easiest on the larger varieties of pumpkins ...

Start small to get the hang of it. Practice on smaller parts like the teeth or eyes before moving on to complete faces.

"Spend some time at it, make it unique and give it character," Farmer Mike says. *"And most important, have fun doing it."* Michael Goldman, "Creative Carving," *Boys' Life*, October 2007

THE POWER OF PARAPHRASING

Not every quote you write in your notebook should be used in your article. There are times when you should paraphrase what someone said—put it in your own words.

In a direct quote (one that uses quotation marks), you must use the words exactly the way the person said them. When you paraphrase, you can choose the words that you use. But while it is OK to change the words, don't change the meaning of the statement.

Paraphrase quotes that are long and hard to understand. Use your words to make it clearer and shorter. If someone tells you a long story, use quotes for the best parts of it. Paraphrase the rest. If someone speaks in incomplete sentences, don't quote them—paraphrase their words instead. If you're giving examples compiled from several sources, as Paula Murphey did in her article, put them together in one paraphrased paragraph. You can add quotes for emphasis.

The Scouts found photographs, a family Bible, videos, personal checks, "everything imaginable," Matt says. During the cleanup, Blake found his Boy Scouts of America popcorn patch. "It's all I have left of my Scout stuff."

Paula Murphey, "Our Friends Needed Us," *Boys' Life*, August 2007

Tips and techniques

Develop your own version of shorthand for note taking so you can quickly write the words people say. For example, use "bc" for because and "wo" for without. You can also use symbols, such as "+" for and, or "#" for number. Use people's initials (JS for Joe Smith, JD for Jane Doe) instead of names. Make sure you remember what the abbreviations stand for, so when you read your quotes to someone or you sit down to write, you know what you meant.

Tips and techniques

Quotes work best when they are spread apart in a story. Try to work them into your narrative instead of putting several quotes together.

CASE STUDY

Paraphrasing can be hard work, Jacqui Banaszynski says, because you have to understand what you heard well enough to translate it in simple language for the reader. "You need to know the essence of what you want to say. You have to boil down your point to its simplest form."

BEAT WRITER'S BLOCK

Even famous writers sometimes get stuck for words or ideas. This is called writer's block.

If you have been following the writer's golden rule (writing regularly and often), you already have some ways to battle writer's block. Here are some of its causes and other weapons to use.

Your inner critic

Try not to listen to that inner voice that might whisper negative ideas about your writing. All writers try out ideas that don't work. Sometimes they keep reworking the same idea until it does work. Sometimes they have to move on to something else. It can help to have an objective person read your article and give you feedback. Don't be afraid to revise your article or to rewrite parts of it entirely. The more you write, the better you will be.

A change of pace

Defeat writer's block by changing your writing habits. If you normally brainstorm sitting still, try walking instead. If you usually like quiet while you write, add music to your article writing zone. If you write at the computer, try pen and paper. If you usually write at home, go to the library. Vary your writing habits for each stage of the process.

CASE STUDY

"When I get writer's block, which is constantly, I grab a friend for coffee or call someone to talk it through," says Jacqui Banaszynski. "I talk about the story and then eventually I hear the story as I talk."

Tips and techniques

If you're battling writer's block, take a break and think about new subjects you'd like to tackle. Read a magazine or a newspaper to see if it sparks any ideas. Maybe you can search for some fun subjects on the Internet. Think of ways to tie your ideas to coming events or to anniversaries of historic happenings.

Now it's your turn

Step lively!

Don't sit still for writer's block. Sometimes even a very simple change of pace helps. Take a break with a walk outdoors, a workout at the gym, or an errand to the store. A short time away from writing may be all you need.

CASE STUDY

Brad Herzog admits that he often battles writer's block. The best way to beat it, he says, is to take a break. "Writing is an interesting job," he says. "It takes a lot of thought. You aren't just stapling things together or something brainless like that. You have to take brain breaks every now and then." Herzog's favorite "brain break" is playing online Scrabble. "I think I might be the best online Scrabble player in history," he jokes.

Today's journalists have many choices of where and how to publish their work.

Besides traditional newspapers and magazines, there are also many opportunities with Internet publications. Kids can also create their own opportunities, whether it is publishing a neighborhood newspaper or creating an online blog about a favorite cause or activity.

"Things are really changing for journalists," Lynn Closway says. "Enter the world of online publications, digital technology, streaming video, 24-hour access to news, interactive video and blogging—potential journalists must be nimble and ready to work their way up through many forms of media."

Writing opportunities

There are a growing number of organizations that offer writing opportunities to young people. Among them is a nonprofit organization for kids in the Indianapolis, Indiana, area known as Y-Press. It encourages students to report and write on local news events as a way to develop leadership skills. It also gives kids a voice in the world.

The Upper Peninsula Children's Museum in Marquette, Michigan, has created a youth news bureau called 8-18 Media. Kids between the ages of 8 and 18 write stories about topics important to them. The stories are published in *Marquette Monthly* magazine and aired on local radio stations.

Put your writing to work

Not every article you write has to be published in a newspaper or magazine or on the Internet. Perhaps your article could be used as a news release to promote a school activity, or to educate people about a charity that you feel strongly about. Charities and other non-profit organizations can always benefit from aspiring writers who are willing to volunteer their time and talents to help. Not only will you get great experience, you will also put your writing to good use.

By the book

Writers rely on many resources when working on an article. It's good to keep those necessary resources, from the phone book to the dictionary, close at hand. They can be in book format or online. Writers also find it helpful to use stylebooks such as *The Associated Press Stylebook* and *The Elements of Style*. Both are well-known guides to writing style and word usage.

A writers group

Writing may seem lonely. Some writers get encouragement by sharing their works-in-progress with other writers. They meet regularly in person or over the Internet with "writing buddies." These groups help fight writer's block by sharing ideas, experiences, and even goals.

NOW WHAT?

Congratulations! Completing an article is a wonderful achievement. You have learned a lot about writing and probably a lot about various people and topics, too. You are now ready to take the next step in a lifetime filled with more story ideas than you can even imagine.

Another article?

Perhaps while researching your article you discovered another subject that fascinates you. Maybe that can become the topic of the next article you write. When Brad Herzog finished a project about the top 100 athletes in U.S. history, he used what he had learned about certain sports myths to start another article for another magazine. "I view each assignment as a sort of mini-education in which I immerse myself in a particular subject," he says. "Information spurs the imagination. One project can lead to another."

Get the beat

At some newspapers and magazines, writers develop a beat—a specific area where they focus their reporting and writing. You can do the same thing. Create your own beat that relates to something you are involved in or that you are passionate about. Volunteer to write about the theater department for your high school newspaper. Or make a habit of writing articles about a school sports team. The more you immerse yourself in a subject, the more story ideas you will find related to that subject.

Start a series

Sometimes one article isn't enough. Some subjects need several articles, or a series of articles, to tell the full story. If you feel your story isn't quite complete even after your article is done, keep writing. A series, however, doesn't have to be limited to a single story idea. As long as there is a

common thread, a series can be almost anything. Perhaps you could write a series of profiles about teachers at your school, or a series of features about student organizations.

Tips and techniques

Be prepared to package your stories for any number of media. A story might appear in full form in a printed publication, but also as a short synopsis on a Web site or in video or audio format on the Internet. "Be prepared to be flexible and to embrace the new world of journalism," says Lynn Closway (left).

LEARN FROM THE WRITERS

You can learn a great deal from the advice of successful writers. Almost all will tell you that hard work and occasional failure are part of the writing lifestyle. Although some writers have full-time jobs with magazines, newspapers, or Web sites, many others work as freelancers, writing articles on assignment.

Brad Herzog

Brad Herzog wrote his first article when he was 14 years old. It was for his high school newspaper. The story, about his experience as a batboy for the Chicago White Sox, was all it took. "The first time I saw my name in the newspaper, I was hooked," he says.

After graduating from Cornell University, where he was able to serve as an intern for *Sports Illustrated Kids*, he worked as a sportswriter at a daily newspaper in Ithaca, New York. After less than two years, however, he left to pursue a freelance writing career on his own. He's been happily doing that for more than 16 years.

Today he writes many articles and books for children. He also visits elementary schools to talk to kids, teachers, and parents about writing. "I tell them to use their kids' passions to get them interested in writing," he says. "For me, it was sports."

Jacqui Banaszynski

Jacqui Banaszynski started writing in a corner of her bedroom closet, where she would craft letters to pen pals as a grade-schooler. That evolved into writing articles for the high school newspaper in her hometown of Pulaski, Wisconsin. The school paper also served as the town's newspaper. "I got involved when I was 14, and I've never looked back," Banaszynski says.

During her more than 30-year career as a journalist, she has worked for several major daily newspapers, including the St. Paul *Pioneer Press* and *The Seattle Times.* In 1988, she won the Pulitzer Prize in feature writing for her series called "AIDS in the Heartland."

Today she teaches journalism at the University of Missouri School of Journalism. She rarely has to write on deadline anymore, but she still appreciates the adrenaline rush that comes with finishing an article. "Not everybody is wired to think under that kind of pressure," she says, "but I find it both extremely difficult and very satisfying."

Meg Moss

Meg Moss has been a freelance writer for almost 25 years. She started her career, however, working in a museum as an anthropologist. But even then, she was a writer. Part of her job was to write the text to go along with the exhibits she helped create.

When a college friend asked if she would be interested in writing articles for an educational magazine the friend was working on, Moss thought it was a natural next move. Now she is the contributing editor for *Ask* magazine, where she is able to combine her love of science and her writing talents. "Putting together a magazine is a lot like putting together an exhibit for a museum," she says. "They both need brevity, conciseness, and a strong visual element."

PREPARE YOUR WORK

Unless you are on deadline, let your article rest on your desk for a few days. When you pick it up to read it through again, you will have fresh eyes to spot any flaws.

Edit your work

Reading your work aloud is one way to make the writing crisper. Now is the time to check spelling and punctuation, too. When the article is as good as it can be, write it again in longhand or type it on the computer.

Think of a headline or title

Great headlines and titles contain more than the subject of the article. It is important to think of an intriguing phrase that describes your article. Think about the headlines you have seen in newspapers and magazines. They are often short and to the point. Sometimes they include humor or a play on words. Have fun thinking about the headline or title for your article.

Tips and techniques
Always make a copy of your article before you give it to others to read. Otherwise, if they lose it, you may have lost all your valuable work.

Be professional

If you have a computer, you can type your article to give it a professional look. Articles should always be printed on one side of white paper, with wide margins and double spacing. Number the pages, and include the headline on the top of each page. At the front, you should have a title page with your name, address, telephone number, and e-mail address. (Repeat this information on the last page.)

Having the article on a computer file also means you can print a copy whenever you need one or revise the whole article if you want to.

Editorial help

When you turn in your article for publication, an editor will take a look at it. An editor makes suggestions for changes and cleans up the writing. Although it might be hard to have someone tell you to change your article, a good editor will work with you to make the final product the best it can be. "An editor is your friend," Meg Moss says. "They are there to help you, to make your writing look good—and to make you look good too."

REACH YOUR AUDIENCE

The next step is to find an audience for your article. Family members or classmates may want to read it. Or you may want to share your work with more people by trying to get it published.

Some places to publish your article

If your article pertains to your school or would be of interest to your classmates, submit it to the school newspaper or magazine. There are also many general interest magazines that accept submissions from young writers. Some give writing advice and run regular competitions. Each publication has its own rules about submitting work, so remember to read these carefully. Watch your local newspaper or look in your favorite magazines for writing competitions you could enter.

Finding a publisher

Study the market to find out which magazines accept article submissions. Addresses of magazine publishers and information about whether they accept submissions can sometimes be found in the magazines themselves and online. They are also in writers handbooks in your library. Keep in mind that articles that haven't been requested or paid for by a publisher —called unsolicited manuscripts—are rarely published. Secure any submission with a staple or paper clip, and always enclose a short letter (explaining what you have sent) and a self-addressed, stamped envelope (an SASE) if you want the article returned.

Writer's tip

Don't lose heart if an editor rejects your article. See this as a chance to make your work better and try again. Remember, having your work published is wonderful, but it is not the only thing. Being able to write an article is an accomplishment that will delight the people you love. Talk about it with your brother or sister. Read it to your grandfather. Find your audience.

Some final words

Writing an article brings you closer to life's many possibilities and problems. It will change you in some way. You will understand more about people and why they behave as they do. You will learn about so many different things. You will develop a sense of curiosity and nose for the news that will keep you searching for stories. You are ready to search out your next scoop!

Read! Write!

And follow the news!

Glossary

blogs—frequently updated online journals, short for Web logs

brevity—shortness

credibility—being reliable and believable

edit—to remove all unnecessary words from your story, correcting errors and rewriting the text until the story is the best it can be

editors—people at a magazine or newspaper who decide which articles will be published; a copy editor corrects errors in punctuation, grammar, and style

first-person viewpoint—viewpoint that allows the writer to tell the story; readers feel as if the writer is talking directly to them

interview—to ask someone questions for the purpose of using the answers in an article

journalists—writers for newspapers, magazines, or other news outlets; journalists report the news by asking the questions who, what, when, where, why, and how

libel—knowingly false written words that damage someone's reputation

manuscripts—books or articles typed or written by hand

metaphor—figure of speech that paints a word picture; calling a man "a mouse" is a metaphor from which we learn in one word that the man is timid or weak, not that he is actually a mouse

narrative—telling of a story

objective—without bias or personal feelings

paraphrase—express the same message in different words

point of view—eyes through which a story is told

publishers—individuals or companies that pay for an author's article to be printed in a magazine or newspaper and that distribute and sell the magazines or newspapers

quote—information from a source in the exact words of the source

shorthand—way of writing rapidly

simile—saying something is like something else; a word picture, such as "clouds like frayed lace"

sources—people, books, articles, or Web sites that provide information for an article

unsolicited manuscripts—manuscripts that are sent to publishers without being requested; these submissions usually end up in the "slush pile," where they may wait a long time to be read

writer's block—when writers think they can no longer write or have used up all their ideas

Further information

Visit your local libraries and make friends with the librarians. They can direct you to useful sources of information, including newspapers and magazines that publish articles written by young people. You can learn your craft and read great stories at the same time. Librarians will also know if any published writers are scheduled to speak in your area.

Many journalists visit schools and offer writing workshops. Ask your teacher to invite a favorite journalist to speak at your school.

On the Web

For more information on this topic, use FactHound.
1. Go to *www.facthound.com*
2. Type in this book ID: 0756538556
3. Click on the *Fetch It* button.
FactHound will find the best Web sites for you.

Read all the Write Your Own books

Write Your Own Adventure Story
Write Your Own Article
Write Your Own Autobiography
Write Your Own Biography
Write Your Own Fairy Tale
Write Your Own Fantasy Story
Write Your Own Folktale
Write Your Own Graphic Novel
Write Your Own Legend
Write Your Own Mystery Story
Write Your Own Myth
Write Your Own Poetry
Write Your Own Realistic Fiction Story
Write Your Own Science Fiction Story
Write Your Own Tall Tale

Read more articles in popular magazines

American Girl
Ask
Boys' Life
Calliope World History for Young People
Cobblestone American History for Kids
Creative Kids
Cricket
Dig
Discovery Girls
Faces
Girls' Life Magazine
Junior Scholastic
Muse
National Geographic Kids
New Moon
Nick Magazine
Odyssey
Owl
Read
Science World
Skipping Stones
Sports Illustrated Kids
Stone Soup
Time for Kids

Articles cited

Alex (last name withheld). "Alex's Story." *American Girl.* April 2008, pp. 27–31.

Braunstein, Sarah. "Ultimate Sports Collections." *Sports Illustrated Kids.* December 2007, pp. G14–G19.

Calkins, Virginia. "Give the People What They Want." *Cobblestone.* December 2007, pp. 26–28.

Goldman, Michael. "Creative Carving." *Boys' Life.* October 2007, pp. 30–33.

Graf, Christine. "Science in a Land of Extremes." *Faces.* May 2006, pp. 24–27.

Gramling, Gary. "In Good Hands." *Sports Illustrated Kids.* December 2007, pp. G4–G8.

Hackl, Abby Christine. "Life in Tunisia." *Faces.* May 2006, pp. 30–33.

Jensen, Sean. "Runaway Success." *Sports Illustrated Kids.* Winter 2007, pp. 16–18.

Keith, Ted. "Peyton Is Your #1." *Sports Illustrated Kids.* December 2007, pp. 20–22.

Lee, Catherine. "Catherine's Page." *Discovery Girls.* February/March 2008, p. 6.

Lopata, Peg. "Paddle Power." *Faces.* May 2007, p. 21.

McCollum, Sean. "Escape to Alcatraz." *Boys' Life.* October 2007, pp. 34–39.

Moss, Meg. "Summer, Winter, Spring, Fall … Night?" *Ask.* October 2007, pp. 6–11.

Moss, Meg. "Survivors." *Muse.* September 2007, p. 40.

Moss, Meg. "Swarm!" *Ask.* May/June 2005, pp. 22–27.

Moss, Meg. "Volcanoes Rock the World." *Ask.* October 2005, pp. 6–12.

Murphey, Paula. "Our Friends Needed Us." *Boys' Life.* August 2007, pp. 16–21.

Musgrave, Ruth. "Decoding DogSpeak." *National Geographic Kids.* March 2006, pp. 26–27.

Pickerill, Martha, ed. "The Farmers' Bank." *Time for Kids.* 7 March 2008, p. 3.

Pickerill, Martha, ed. "The Power of Music." *Time for Kids.* 7 March 2008, p. 3.

Risch, Dan. "Life at the Top." *Faces.* May 2006, pp. 16–17.

Wells, Alex. "Guest Review: *Shanghai Messenger.*" *Faces.* May 2007, p. 47.

White, Kelly. "Triple Threat." *Girls' Life Magazine.* February/March 2008, p. 36.

Image credits

Index